BIGFOOT

By Marty Erickson

Published by The Child's World®
1980 Lookout Drive • Mankato, MN 56003-1705
800-599-READ • www.childsworld.com

Photographs ©: Shutterstock Images, cover (Bigfoot), 1 (Bigfoot), 7, 20, 21, 23, 24; Tom Tom/Shutterstock Images, cover (background), 1–3 (background); Paul Juser/Shutterstock Images, 5, 6, 12; iStockphoto, 9; Oliver Denker/Shutterstock Images, 10; Ferenc Szelepcsenyi/Shutterstock Images, 13; Daniel Eskridge/Shutterstock Images, 15; Rudy Riva/Shutterstock Images, 16; Bettmann/Getty Images, 19

Copyright © 2022 by The Child's World®
All rights reserved. No part of this book may be reproduced or utilized in any form or by any means without written permission from the publisher.

ISBN 9781503850279 (Reinforced Library Binding)
ISBN 9781503850750 (Portable Document Format)
ISBN 9781503851511 (Online Multi-user eBook)
LCCN 2021939343

Printed in the United States of America

Table of CONTENTS

CHAPTER ONE

Tracks in the Mud...4

CHAPTER TWO

A Missing Link...8

CHAPTER THREE

Big and Hairy...14

CHAPTER FOUR

The Search Continues...18

Glossary...22

To Learn More...23

Index...24

CHAPTER ONE

Tracks in the Mud

The ground beneath the team's feet was soft. Brown leaves covered the soil. A recent rainstorm had left areas of squishy mud. The researchers were investigating claims of Bigfoot tracks. A **witness** led the team through the forest. He had seen the tracks first.

Birds chirped in the treetops. Finally, the team stopped. The ground looked different here. Leaves were shoved away. The team saw a large track pressed into the mud. One member squatted down. He tried to get a better look.

Some people believe that a legendary creature called Bigfoot lives deep within the forests of North America.

The researcher saw the print of a big toe. There were a few other toeprints visible. Team members talked with each other. It was a convincing track. Part of another print could be seen in the mud, too.

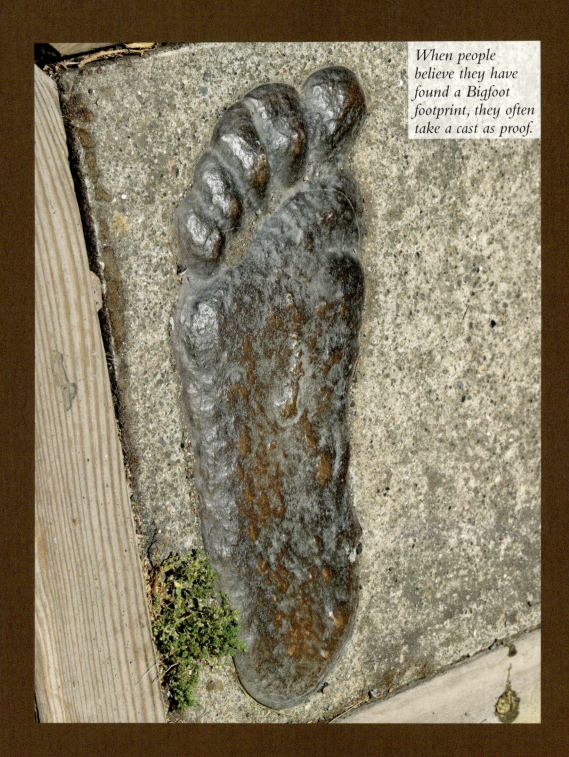

When people believe they have found a Bigfoot footprint, they often take a cast as proof.

The researchers took out plaster. They made a **cast** of the track. When the plaster hardened, the team could see the details of the track more clearly. One person measured the footprint. It appeared to be more than 18 inches (46 cm) long. No one in the group had a good explanation for the track. It did not belong to a bear. The researchers believed they had found **evidence** of Bigfoot.

Bigfoot is said to be a large, hairy, humanlike creature. Stories say it roams forests and **remote** areas in North America. Legends of a Bigfoot-like creature exist around the world. There are many similarities between the stories.

CHAPTER TWO

A MISSING LINK

Communities around the world have legends of a Bigfoot-like creature. Stories around the world are different. Each place has a different name for the creature.

Several Native American tribes have Bigfoot legends. In the United States, the creature is often called Bigfoot or Sasquatch. The name *Sasquatch* comes from the Sts'ailes, a First Nation in Canada. This nation tells stories of *Sasq'ets*, which means "wild man."

Stories of Bigfoot-like creatures have been told throughout history.

Stories about the Yeti often say it is white, like snow.

Bigfoot legends are common in other parts of the world. One of the most famous examples is the Yeti. It is also known as the Abominable Snowman. The myth of the Yeti comes from people living in the Himalayas. These are tall, snow-covered mountains in southern Asia. Mount Everest, the tallest mountain above sea level on Earth, is in the Himalayas.

   In Australia, Aboriginal peoples tell stories of the Yowie. The Yowie lives in the backcountry of Australia. Both the Yeti and Yowie are large, hairy creatures like Sasquatch.

There are many Bigfoot museums across the United States. One is in Willow Creek, California.

There are several **theories** about what Bigfoot is. Some people consider it to be a lost member of the primate family. The primate family includes monkeys, apes, and humans. Other researchers believe Bigfoot may be the last of the Neanderthals. Neanderthals were prehistoric humans. They lived before modern humans.

Dr. Jane Goodall is famous for studying chimpanzees and other primates. She has said she believes Bigfoot could exist.

CHAPTER THREE
BIG AND HAIRY

Legends describe Bigfoot as tall and strong. Most stories say Bigfoot is 6 to 15 feet (1.8 to 4.6 m) tall. Legends say Bigfoot is covered in hair. People say Bigfoot's hair can be black, brown, gray, or white.

As its name suggests, Bigfoot is said to have large feet. Some people claim they have found Bigfoot's footprints. Those tracks measure up to 2 feet (0.6 m) long. That is much bigger than the average human footprint.

humanlike face

hairy body

People think Bigfoot is a tall, humanlike creature that lives in heavily forested areas.

6 to 15 feet (1.8 to 4.6 m) tall

After many people claimed to have seen Bigfoot along the Pikes Peak Highway in Colorado, this sign was installed.

People believe Bigfoot is a shy creature. They think it might live alone or in a small family group. Stories of Bigfoot say it lives in remote areas. They say it lives in mountains and forests. These areas give the creature places to hide.

People search for Bigfoot. Some say they have heard it. They say Bigfoot makes grunts or growling sounds. Some people also say that Bigfoot has a bad smell.

CHAPTER FOUR

THE SEARCH CONTINUES

Bigfoot continues to fascinate people. North America is home to research organizations and Bigfoot festivals. People have even made TV shows and movies about Bigfoot. Investigators search for evidence of Bigfoot.

In addition to looking for new evidence, researchers **analyze** past evidence. There are many footprints. People can look at the plaster casts. Researchers also look at films that claim to show Bigfoot. For example, in 1967, people said they captured Bigfoot on video. Researchers continue to study the video. Many people regard the film as one of the best pieces of evidence for Bigfoot.

In 1967, rodeo riders Roger Patterson and Bob Gimlin took a famous video that supposedly showed Bigfoot. Many people consider the Patterson-Gimlin film to be proof that Bigfoot exists.

Looking at past photos and videos helps people figure out what could be real. Many photos and videos have been **debunked**. Some footprints turned out to be **hoaxes**.

There are many people who do not believe Bigfoot exists. They say people are most likely seeing black bears. Black bears are common in the Pacific Northwest of the United States. When black bears stand up, they can look humanlike.

Black bears can stand on two feet, giving them an almost humanlike appearance.

Though there is no definitive proof that Bigfoot exists, many people still believe.

Bigfoot continues to capture people's imaginations. People may never know the truth. But that won't stop them from trying to find answers.

GLOSSARY

analyze (AN-uh-lyz) To analyze something means to study it. Researchers analyze photos and videos to see if they could possibly show Bigfoot.

cast (KAST) A cast is a 3D copy of an indentation or mold. The researchers made a cast of the Bigfoot tracks.

debunked (dee-BUNKT) Something is debunked when it is proved to be false. Several photos people claimed were of Bigfoot were debunked.

evidence (EH-vuh-dunss) Evidence is a piece of information that helps researchers understand a question. Researchers look for evidence of Bigfoot, such as tracks.

hoaxes (HOHKSS-es) Hoaxes are events or objects that have been faked. Some Bigfoot tracks turned out to be hoaxes.

remote (reh-MOHT) A place is remote when it is far from towns or cities. Legends say Bigfoot lives in remote areas.

theories (THEER-eez) Theories are guesses of what the cause of something may be. Some theories about Bigfoot say it is a lost primate species.

witness (WITT-ness) A witness is a person who sees an event. The witness saw Bigfoot tracks and led the research team to the tracks.

TO LEARN MORE

In the Library

Halls, Kelly Milner. *Cryptid Creatures: A Field Guide.* Seattle, WA: Little Bigfoot, 2019.

Kallio, Jamie. *Bigfoot.* Mankato, MN: The Child's World, 2016.

Peabody, Erin. *Bigfoot.* New York, NY: Little Bee, 2017.

On the Web

Visit our website for links about Bigfoot:

childsworld.com/links

Note to Parents, Teachers, and Librarians: We routinely verify our Web links to make sure they are safe and active sites. So encourage your readers to check them out!

INDEX

appearance, 7, 11, 14
Australia, 11

bears, 7, 20
behavior, 17

casts, 7, 18

footprints, 4–7, 14, 18–20

Himalayas, 11

North America, 7, 8

primates, 12

Sts'ailes, 8

Yeti, 11
Yowie, 11

ABOUT THE AUTHOR

Marty Erickson is a writer living in Minnesota. They write books for young people full time and like to go hiking.